Lazy Len

Traditional tale adapted by Gill Munton
Series Editor: Louis Fidge

Contents

Lenny

Larry

Sam

Lazy Lenny

This is Lenny.

Maa! Maa! Maa!

This is Lenny's goat.

Every day, Lenny fed the goat.
But Lenny did not like hard work.
He was lazy.

Lenny had an idea.
He went to see Larry.

Lenny said, 'You have got a goat and
I have got a goat.
You can live with me in my big house.
Then you can look after two goats!'

Larry said, 'That's a good idea.'

So Larry and his goat
went to live with Lenny.
Every day, Larry fed the two goats.
Every day, he milked them.
But Larry was lazy, too!

Larry had an idea.

He said, 'We can sell the goats.
We can buy some bees!'

Lenny said, 'That's a good idea.
Bees make honey. We can sell the honey!'

Lenny and Larry took the goats to the farm.

'Can we sell the goats?
Can we buy some bees?' they said.

The farmer said, 'Yes, you can.'

Lenny and Larry were happy.
The bees made lots of honey.
Lenny and Larry did not work at all.

Lenny said, 'Look! The honey pot is full!'

The next day, the honey pot was empty!
Lenny said, 'Where is the honey?'

'You ate the honey, Larry!
We cannot sell it now!
What can we do?'

13

Lenny had an idea.

He said, 'We can sell the bees.
We can buy some sheep!'

Larry said, 'That's a good idea!
Sheep give us wool.'

Lenny said, 'We can ask Sam to live with us.
He can look after the sheep.'

Lenny and Larry took the bees to the farm.

'Can we sell the bees?
Can we buy some sheep?' they said.

The farmer said, 'Yes, you can.'

Lenny and Larry were happy.
Sam looked after the sheep.
The sheep gave lots of wool.
Lenny and Larry did not work at all.

But Sam was lazy, too!

I don't like hard work.

Baa! Baa!

Lenny said to Sam,
'Please mend the fence.'

Sam said, 'Yes, Lenny.'

But Sam was lazy.
He did not mend the fence.

The next day, Lenny said,
'Where are the sheep?
You went to sleep, Sam.'

Larry said, 'The sheep ran away!
What can we do?'

Lenny said, 'Sam is lazy! He can go!'

Larry said, 'We haven't got any goats.
We haven't got any bees
and we haven't got any sheep.'

Lenny said, 'We can buy two goats.
And we can both look after them!'

Now Lenny and Larry work hard.
The two goats give milk and cheese.
They sell the milk and cheese.
Lenny and Larry are happy!

Maa! Maa! Maa!
The goats gave milk and cheese.
But Larry and Lenny were lazy,
They sold them for some bees.

Buzz! Buzz! Buzz!
The honey was in a pot.
But now the pot is empty,
Larry ate the lot!

Baa! Baa! Baa!
The sheep grew lots of wool.
Lenny and Larry sold it,
Three bags full.

Baa! Baa! Baa!
It was not a happy day.
Sam was very lazy,
And the sheep ran away.

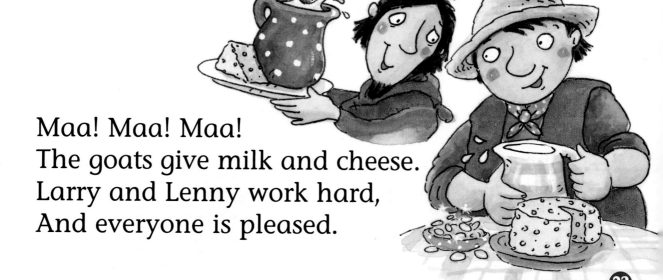

Maa! Maa! Maa!
The goats give milk and cheese.
Larry and Lenny work hard,
And everyone is pleased.

Word list

a	can	good	Lenny	please	too
after	cannot	got	like	pot	took
all	cheese	had	live	ran	two
an	day	happy	look	said	us
and	did	hard	looked	Sam	very
any	do	have	lots	see	was
are	don't	haven't	Maa!	sell	we
ask	empty	he	made	sheep	went
at	every	his	make	sleep	were
ate	farm	honey	me	so	what
away	farmer	house	mend	some	where
Baa!	fed	I	milk	that's	with
bees	fence	idea	milked	the	wool
big	full	in	my	them	work
both	gave	is	next	then	yes
but	give	it	not	they	you
buy	go	Larry	now	this	
Buzz!	goat(s)	lazy	of	to	

Language structures

Past simple tense:
was/were, said, fed, took, made,
did, ate, milked, went, had,
looked, ran, gave

can:
You can live with me.
Can we buy some sheep?

some/any:
We can buy some bees.
We haven't got any goats.

like + noun:
I don't like hard work.
Lenny did not like hard work.

Time phrases:
The next day... / Now... / Every day...

Adjectives:
lazy, hard, happy